For Isobel – there's beauty in numbers – C.S.

For Baby, Babas and Manuel – X.A.

BIG PICTURE PRESS

First published in the UK in 2019 by Big Picture Press,
an imprint of Bonnier Books UK,
The Plaza, 535 King's Road, London, SW10 0SZ
www.templarco.co.uk/big-picture-press
www.bonnierbooks.co.uk

Text copyright © 2019 by Colin Stuart
Illustration copyright © 2019 by Ximo Abadía
Design copyright © 2019 by Big Picture Press

1 3 5 7 9 10 8 6 4 2

All rights reserved

ISBN 978-1-78741-407-5

This book was typeset in Ulissa and BSKombat.
The illustrations were created with graphite,
wax and ink, and coloured digitally.

Edited by Carly Blake and Joanna McInerney
Designed by Adam Allori and Kieran Hood
Production Controller Emma Kidd

Printed in Malaysia

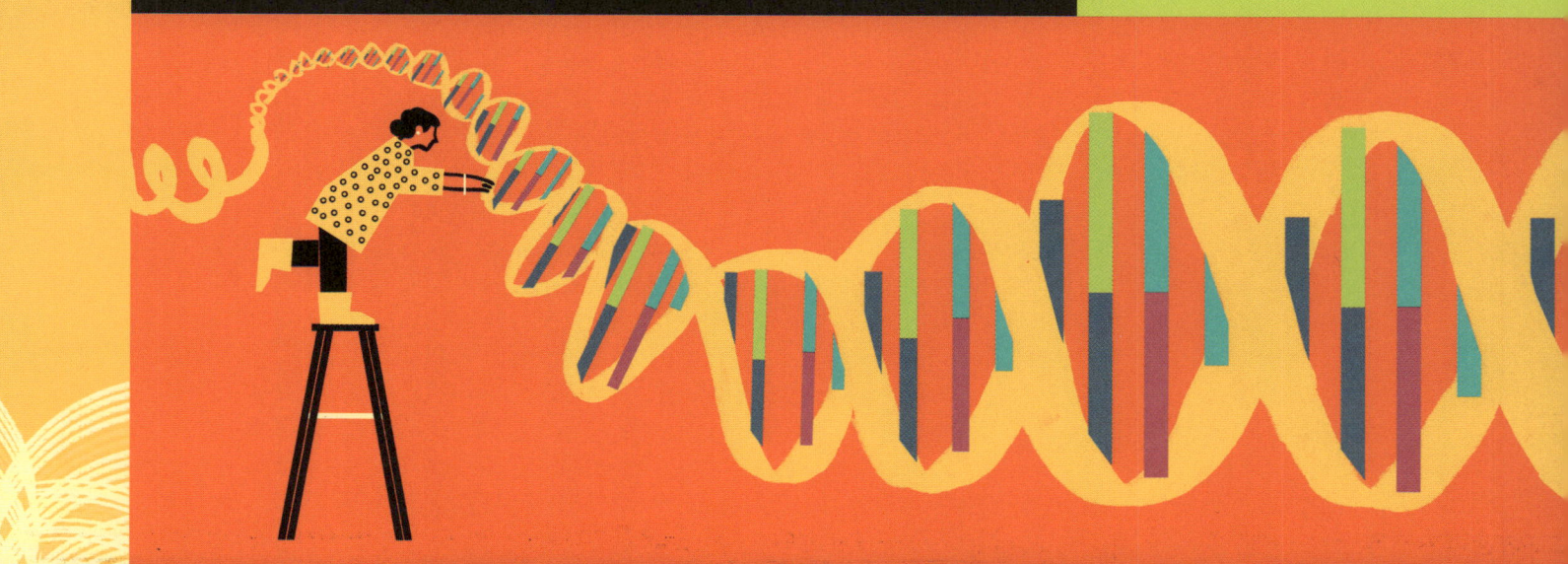

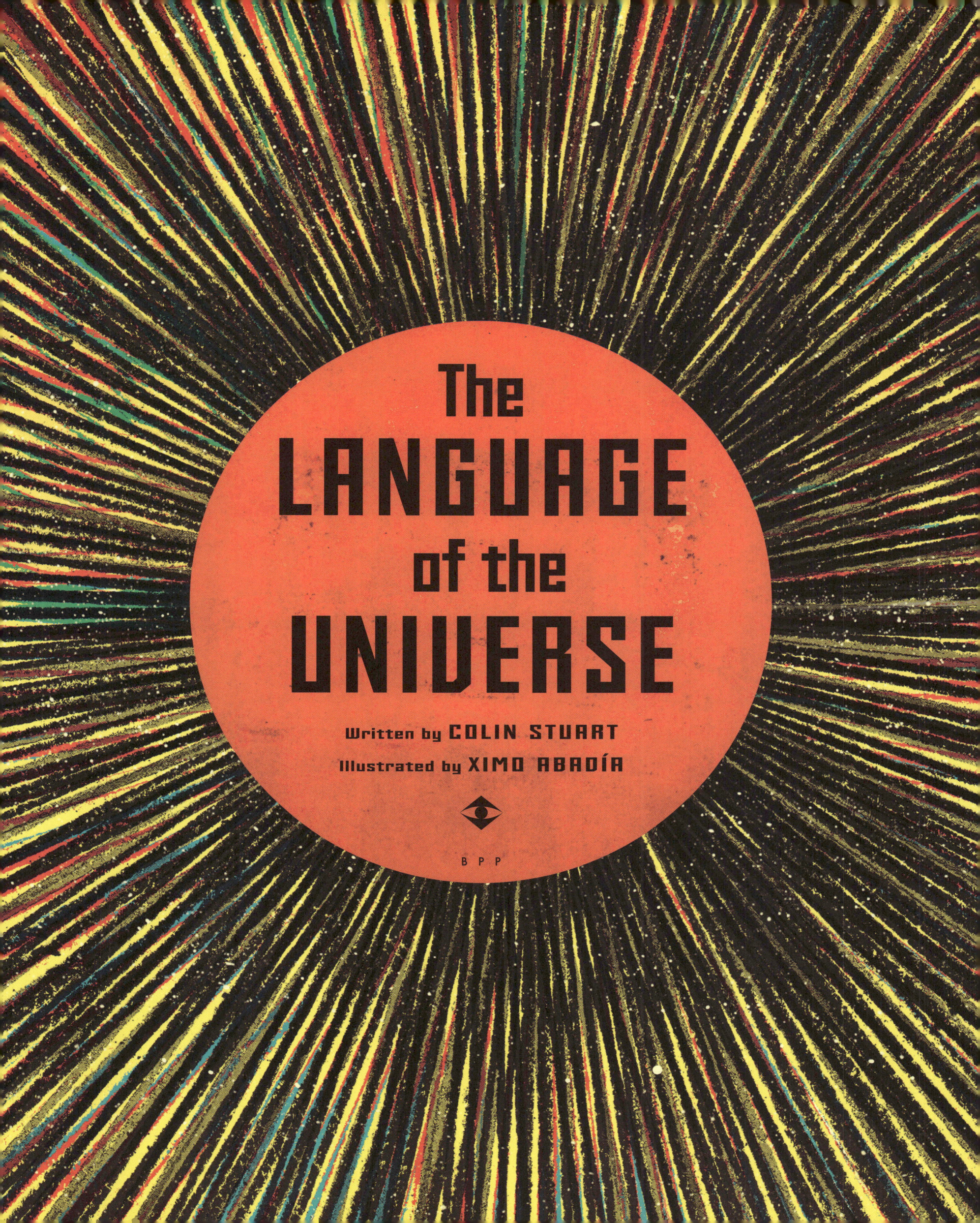

The LANGUAGE of the UNIVERSE

Written by COLIN STUART
Illustrated by XIMO ABADÍA

BPP

The Language of the Universe	8
Our History with Numbers	10

MATHS IN THE NATURAL WORLD

Finding Fibonacci	12
Protecting Yourself with Primes	14
In Search of the Symmetrical	16
Fun with Fractals	18
Teamwork with Tessellation	20
Packing the Perimeter	22
The Platonic Protozoa	24
Getting to Grips with Geometry	26
The Awesome Ant	28
Animal Addition	30
Created from Chromosomes	32
Natural Selection Basics	34

PHYSICS, CHEMISTRY AND ENGINEERING

The Amazing Atom	36
Atom Patterns and the Periodic Table	38
Getting the Hang of Half-Lifes	40
Learning the Laws of Gases	42
Thinking About Time	44
Einstein's Energetic Equation	46
The Secrets of Circuits	48
Playing with Pendulums and Springs	50
The Physics of Floating	52
How to Lift with Levers	54
Putting Pythagoras into Practice	56
Reflecting on Refraction	58

SPACE

Kepler's Clockwork Planets	60
Nailing Gravity with Newton	62
Hurtling Through Space with Hubble	64
Dealing with Distances in Space	66

TECHNOLOGY

Let's Talk Technological Change	68
Calculating with Computers	70
Getting Crafty with Cryptography	72
Building the Future with Big Data	74
The World Needs You	76

The Language of the Universe

Maths can be bamboozling. With all its symbols and letters, it looks like it's written in another language – and it is. **MATHEMATICS is the Language of the Universe**. Numbers are like words, plusses and minuses are like full stops and commas, and equations are like sentences. The greatest poets, authors and playwrights light up the world with their beautiful arrangements of words. Yet, when it comes to maths, the Universe is a better writer than all of them combined. Even Shakespeare had nothing on Nature.

2B +¬ 2B

HAMLET

As you go about your life each day, everything around you is buzzing with maths. The Language of the Universe is sown with every seed, commanded with every computer click and bustles with every breath. Numbers, symbols and equations are the invisible mechanism making every single thing around you tick like an unseen clock.

Maths is arguably the most understood language in the world. It doesn't matter if you speak Chinese, Spanish, English or Swahili, the language of maths is universal. Learn it and you'll soon see the wonder of the Universe come to light as you never have before.

Our History with Numbers

Humans have been using numbers for tens of thousands of years, since around the same time that we learnt how to speak. In the 1970s, archaeologists discovered an ancient baboon leg bone in South Africa and someone had clearly carved 29 marks into it, perhaps to count the days of the phases of the Moon. The bone and its marks are over 40,000 years old – it shows just how long humans have been adding up.

Fast forward to the twenty-first century and we've mastered maths like never before. Numbers are the beating heart of the Internet, computer games and the latest technological wonders. Recent medical treatments, movie special effects and the latest pop songs would all be impossible without maths.

Historically, maths was also a way for people to trade. Understanding if swapping one pig for two goats is a good deal is difficult unless you know numbers. Over time, ancient civilisations from Sumeria, Babylonia and Egypt explored maths more deeply and used their new understanding to invent money and build impressive temples and pyramids. From around 600 BC the ancient Greeks became obsessed with shapes and numbers, and mathematicians such as **PYTHAGORAS** made many of the discoveries you still learn at school today.

Yet maths is far from finished. There are some mathematical puzzles so fiendish that there's a reward of $1 million if you can solve them. Could you be a maths millionaire?

Finding Fibonacci

The natural world is awash with maths. From armadillos to pine cones, animals and plants secretly use numbers in their fight for survival every single day.

Take a closer look at the beautiful sunflower. The seeds in the centre are **arranged in spiral patterns**. Count the number of spirals in a clockwise direction, then the number in an anticlockwise direction…

You should get the answers 21 and 34. These numbers are incredibly special because they are part of one of the most famous sequences in maths: the FIBONACCI SEQUENCE. It is named after an Italian mathematician who lived around 1200. To recreate this number pattern all you have to do is **add up the previous two numbers**. It starts with 1,1. So the next number is 2 (1 + 1), then 3 (1 + 2), followed by 5 (2 + 3). If you keep going you'll end up with:
1, 1, 2, 3, 5, 8, 13, 21, 34, 55 and so on.

21 clockwise spirals + **34 anticlockwise spirals** =

Using the Fibonacci sequence is the best way to **pack as many seeds as possible into a limited amount of space.** It's not just the sunflower that exploits this. Try counting the number of spirals on a pine cone or pineapple. What about the number of petals on a daisy, marigold or buttercup? They all follow this sequence.

Protecting Yourself with Primes

The forests of the Eastern United States are the stage for a most remarkable event. For 13 long years winged insects called **CICADAS** patiently live underground, even though they are fully grown after just eight. Then, suddenly, they all burst out of the ground together to feast on the surrounding trees, find mates, and lay their eggs. Within weeks the baby cicadas burrow back underground, where they spend the next 13 years growing and waiting their turn.

Why are these bugs so patient? It's all to do with **PRIME NUMBERS**. A prime number is one that can **only be divided by two numbers: 1 and itself**. The sequence of prime numbers goes: **2, 3, 5, 7, 11, 13, 17** and so on. Different cicada groups are known to emerge every 7, 13 or 17 years – all prime numbers.

It's thought they do this to help protect themselves from predators. If the cicadas emerged every 12 years then they could be eaten by creatures with life cycles of 2, 3, 4 and 6 years (all of which divide into 12). By surfacing on a prime number year, the cicadas give themselves the best chance of dodging predators, because no other animals – except themselves and those with yearly life cycles – will be expecting their appearance.

2, 3, 5, 7 11, 13, 17

It's not only in nature where using prime numbers is useful for protection. Computer programmers also use them to keep our online data secure (page 72).

In Search of the Symmetrical

Mathematicians love to explore **SYMMETRY**. If an object has **the property of symmetry, it can be rotated or flipped and still look exactly the same**. There are some fascinating examples in the natural world.

Both a starfish and snowflake have what mathematicians call **ROTATIONAL SYMMETRY** – **if you turn them by a certain amount they don't look any different**. How many different ways can you turn a starfish without changing its appearance?

72°

The answer is **five**, so a mathematician would say it has **FIVE-FOLD SYMMETRY**. There are 360 degrees in a circle, so you have to turn the starfish **72 degrees** each time to reach the next matching position. What about a stunning snowflake? How would you describe its symmetry and how many degrees do you have to turn it each time?

?

Answer: Six-fold symmetry, 60 degrees

16

mirror line

REFLECTION SYMMETRY occurs a lot in the animal kingdom. When a butterfly's wings are open you can see that **one half is the mirror image of the other**. The **line that divides each symmetrical half** is called the **MIRROR LINE**.

Shapes that aren't symmetrical are known as **ASYMMETRICAL**. Scientific studies have shown that humans often find **symmetrical faces more beautiful than asymmetrical ones**.

17

Fun with Fractals

Maths doesn't get much prettier than a FRACTAL. These **beautiful never-ending patterns have copies of themselves hidden within them** – zoom in or out and you'll see the same shape repeated over and over again.

Take a look at this fern. One of the side branches is just a miniature version of the whole plant. Look even more closely and you'll see that a side branch of that side branch is also the same!

Fractals are found all over the natural world, from winding rivers to forked lightning. Scientists have even revealed the presence of fractals inside the human body. Your bones are made of two substances called **COLLAGEN** and **APATITE**, which are arranged in a pattern that makes your skeleton particularly strong. Photographs taken of this structure with a powerful microscope show that this pattern repeats in a similar way to a fractal, down to a billionth of a metre.

It's not hard to see why fractals crop up a lot in nature. As living things grow, it is easy for them to make a different sized version of something they've already made before. It's the same design, just repeated on a larger or smaller scale.

Teamwork with Tessellation

Some of the most famous animals on the planet avoid getting eaten by using a clever trick based on the mathematical idea of TESSELLATION. A tessellation is **a repeating pattern of shapes arranged close together without overlapping or leaving gaps**. Fill an empty area with a smaller tessellating shape, such as a square, triangle or diamond, and it's harder to see the individual tiles.

Zebras use a similar technique to confuse predators. Their distinctive BLACK AND WHITE STRIPES mean that it is **harder for a hungry lion to pick out an individual from a herd**. Other creatures try to **remain hidden by blending in with with their surroundings** such as trees or snowy ground. Scientists call this CAMOUFLAGE. The **green baron caterpillar** is a master of this art, seemingly disappearing as soon as it settles on a leaf.

Then there are the animals who use tessellation differently – to warn off anyone who might consider making them lunch, and these ones tend to be **dangerous**. A good example is the highly venomous **CORAL SNAKE**. Its skin is made of brightly coloured bands that are tessellated together, forming a repeating pattern that signals danger.

Packing the Perimeter

Have you ever packed a suitcase with clothes before going on a trip? If you have, you'll know some ways waste more room than others. You'd do well to take a lesson in space-saving from the honeybee – Nature's expert packer.

Bees skillfully construct their homes from honeycomb, which is made out of a wax produced by their bodies. Their building block of choice is the **HEXAGON**. Why this **six-sided shape** and not a triangle or a circle? It's **the best way to fill an area with the same shape without any gaps**. This means the bees can build their homes in the quickest time using the least amount of wax and get the most amount of storage space. People have marvelled at the work of the bee for centuries, but it took until 1998 for mathematician **THOMAS HALES** to officially prove there was no better way of packing space.

TRIANGLES	SQUARES	PENTAGONS	HEXAGONS
✗	✗	✗	✓

Today, scientists and engineers have taken inspiration from the honeybee to help them see further into space. The largest telescopes in the world have huge mirrors made up of hexagonal tiles, arranged like a honeycomb. This is an example of **BIOMIMETICS** – **mimicking (copying) an idea from an animal or plant and using it to improve engineering design**.

mirror

photo of a nebula

23

The Platonic Protozoa

The natural world is teeming with living things on a scale too small for your eyes to see. In your own body there are more **tiny microorganisms** called **BACTERIA** than your own cells! They're so small that more than 100 sitting side-by-side would fit across the full stop at the end of this sentence. This microscopic universe has a beautiful link to maths.

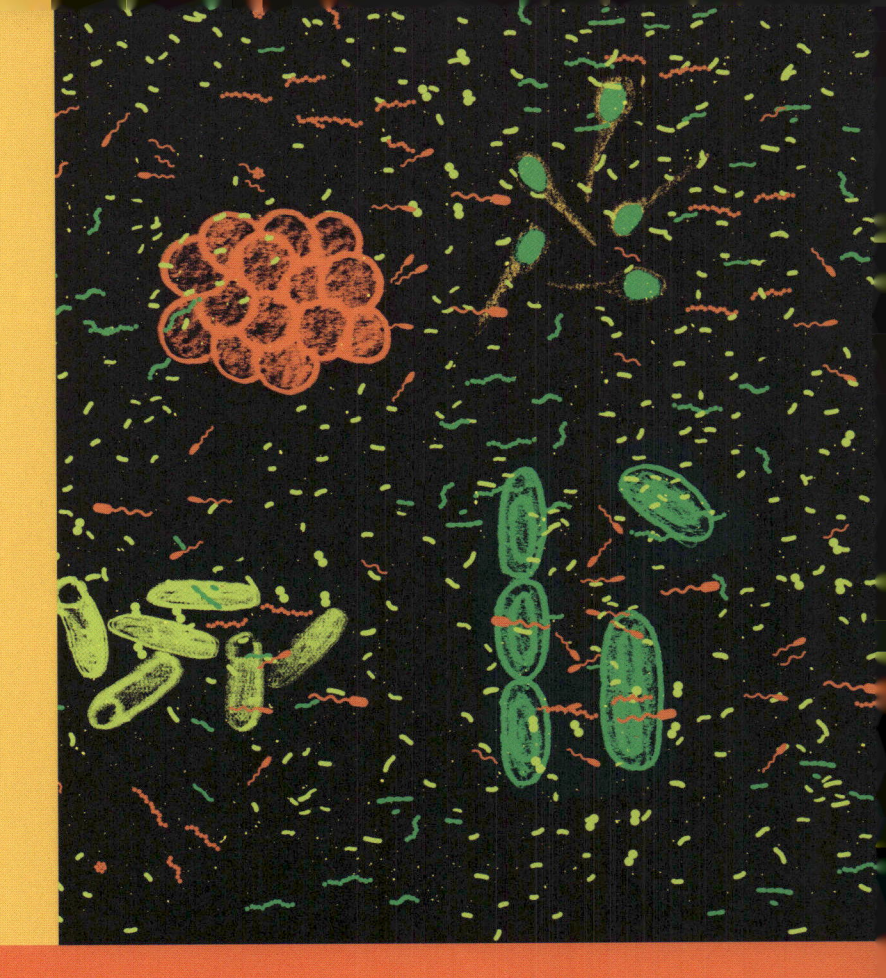

Circoporus octahedrus *Circogonia icosahedra* *Circorrhegma dodecahedra*

Bacteria are joined in this tiny realm by organisms called **PROTOZOA**. They do a lot of the things animals do: eat, reproduce and move – they even communicate with each other. In 1904, German biologist **ERNST HAECKEL** noticed that these tiny living creatures look like a group of shapes called **PLATONIC SOLIDS**.

More recently, biologists have discovered that **many viruses also have an icosahedral structure**.

The **PLATONIC SOLIDS** are a special group of three-dimensional shapes. Their faces are made of the same regular two-dimensional shape. A regular shape is one where all the sides and angles are equal. There are only five Platonic solids: **TETRAHEDRON**, **CUBE**, **OCTAHEDRON**, **DODECAHEDRON** and **ICOSAHEDRON**.

The shapes appear in the scientific names of the protozoa Haeckel described: *Circoporus octahedrus*, *Circogonia icosahedra* and *Circorrhegma dodecahedra*.

Tetrahedron
4 triangular faces

Cube
6 square faces

Octahedron
8 triangular faces

Dodecahedron
12 pentagonal faces

Icosahedron
20 triangular faces

Getting to Grips with Geometry

When it comes to love, maths can be the difference between finding a mate or not – at least if you're a member of the animal kingdom. The name of the game is **GEOMETRY** – **the study of points, lines and the shapes they make**. Mathematician and astronomer Johannes Kepler once said "Where there is matter, there is geometry".

One of the most famous users of geometry is the male peacock, with its bright, shimmering tail that features a pattern of colourful eyespots. Growing such an impressive fan of feathers takes many steps and things can go wrong at any stage. If the geometry of the male's pattern isn't perfect it can be a sign to a potential mate that they are not healthy and are best avoided.

Female great tit birds that have more geometrically perfect white patches on their cheeks are known to breed earlier than their less mathematically pleasing counterparts.

However, the unrivalled king of geometry is the male **WHITE-SPOTTED PUFFERFISH**. Despite being just 12 centimetres long, it creates a large geometric pattern in the sand on the sea floor up to 2 metres wide. Females inspect the patterns, before choosing the most skilled architect as their mate.

The Awesome Ant

Watching a colony of ants can be hypnotic. They are the ultimate team players, all working together for the survival of the group. They're also excellent mathematicians and use their number-crunching skills when looking for a new place to live.

scout

Imagine an ant colony grows too big for its nest. The ants need to find a bigger home to move into. A few scouts are sent out to look for new digs, but how do they decide which is the biggest? After all, they don't have a tape measure to hand.

This discovery was first calculated by French mathematician **GEORGES LOUIS LECLERC** in the 1700s. He worked out the probability of random lines crossing by throwing bread baguettes on to a floor made of planks and recording when they landed over a crack. Ants have been shown to 'count' the **INTERSECTIONS** of their trails and use that to pick the biggest homes for their colony. Clever stuff! Particularly for a creature with a brain a million times small than a human's.

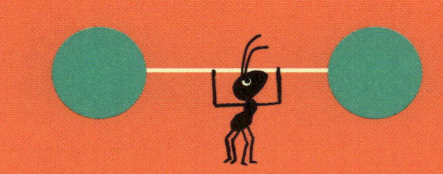

The ants use **GEOMETRY**. During a scout's first visit to a new nest they cross the area several times, leaving lines of chemical trails on the ground. Later, they return for a second look, but this time they don't leave a trail. Instead, they sniff out when they cross the trails they left before. **An ant's path with INTERSECT (cross) a previous trail more often in a small area than in a large area.**

HOME SWEET HOME

Animal Addition

If you think that humans are the only animals that can add up, think again. Scientists have observed a wide range of species doing sums with numbers.

In one experiment, scientists tested the mathematical skills of three-day-old chickens. Scientists set up two screens and the chicks watched as they put 1 ball behind the first screen and 4 balls behind the second. Almost all chicks moved to the screen with the most balls.

That was only half the game. The scientists then removed 2 of the 4 balls and put them behind the first screen. So the first screen now had 3 balls and the second had 2. The young chicks had to work out the sums 4 - 2 and 2 + 1. Amazingly, 80 per cent of chicks correctly moved to the screen with 3 balls.

1 + 1 = 2

Being good at addition and subtraction can really pay off in the animal kingdom. From hunting to finding a mate, animals use maths in a number of different ways to aid their survival. Gorillas, dolphins, elephants, birds and fish are just some of the animals that are naturals when it comes to numbers.

?

85

!

It's not only animals that can count. Scientists have discovered that the insect-eating plant the **Venus fly trap** can keep track of how many times it's been touched by a bug. Each time, the trap gets tighter and tighter, dooming the insect inside.

1

6

10

Created from Chromosomes

Many living things – including humans – are the children of two parents. **A set of instructions for how to make the child** are passed on in the form of **GENES**. Each person has two copies of every gene, one from each parent.

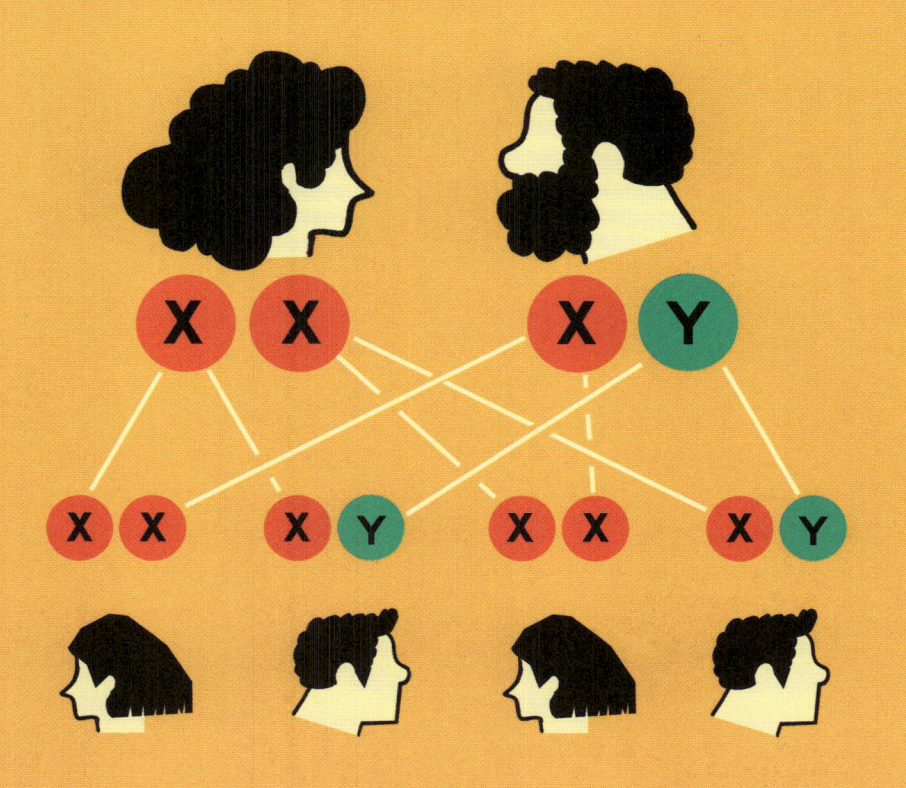

cell

chromosome

nucleus

Among many other things, genes helped determine whether you were born a boy or a girl. Genes are collected together into **structures** called **CHROMOSOMES**. The chromosomes that are linked to whether you're born a boy or a girl are given the letters **X** and **Y**. Though there are some variations, genetically you can either be **female (XX)** or **male (XY)**. Everyone has an X chromosome from their mother. If you were born a boy, your father gave you a **Y CHROMOSOME**. If you were born a girl, your father gave you an **X CHROMOSOME**.

That means there's always a **50:50 probability** of a baby being a boy or a girl. You can see this by drawing a special grid called a PUNNETT SQUARE, named after British biologist REGINALD PUNNETT. It shows all four potential combinations.

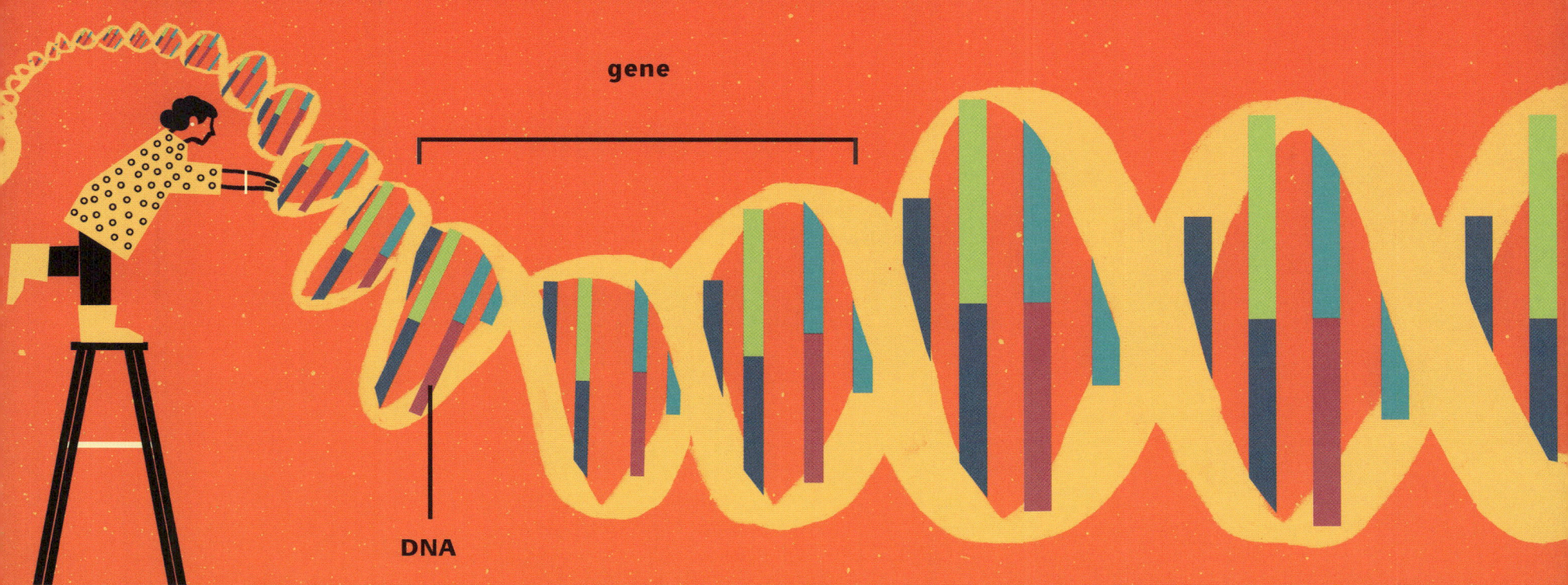

It doesn't matter if a woman has given birth to three boys already, there's still an even chance her fourth child will be a girl.

Natural Selection Basics

The natural world is an amazing place full of awe and wonder. If you're not careful, though, you might get the wrong idea about how it works. You might congratulate the bee for being so clever as to work out the right shape to make its honeycomb, celebrate the sunflower for the smart way it sorts its seeds or commend the cicada for avoiding being eaten.

In truth it wasn't a decision made by the bee, flower or bug – it was a mistake. CHARLES DARWIN famously published a very important book called **On the Origin of Species** in 1859, in which he wrote about a process called NATURAL SELECTION. Whenever a living thing passes on its genes, the information is never copied perfectly, and the child is slightly different from its parents. These small mistakes are called MUTATIONS.

Some mutations, such as learning how to build a better home, being able to escape from predators or finding a new source of food, are an improvement, which helps the organism survive. When that organism has children, the genetic advantage is passed on. Other times, mutations are not helpful and the creature cannot survive to pass it on.

Over many generations the best mutations are mutated even further, until Nature has **accidentally calculated the best mathematical way to do something**. For example, the Morgan's sphinx moth's long mouthpart is exactly the right size to drink nectar from Darwin's orchid flower and the giraffe's long neck is just right to reach high leafy branches. So making mistakes isn't always a bad thing – some of the most perfect things on the planet are the result of them!

Morgan's sphinx moth

The Amazing Atom

Everything in the Universe, from planets to people to paper, is made up of **tiny building blocks** called ATOMS. Each atom has a centre known as the NUCLEUS, with particles called ELECTRONS orbiting it like planets circling around the Sun.

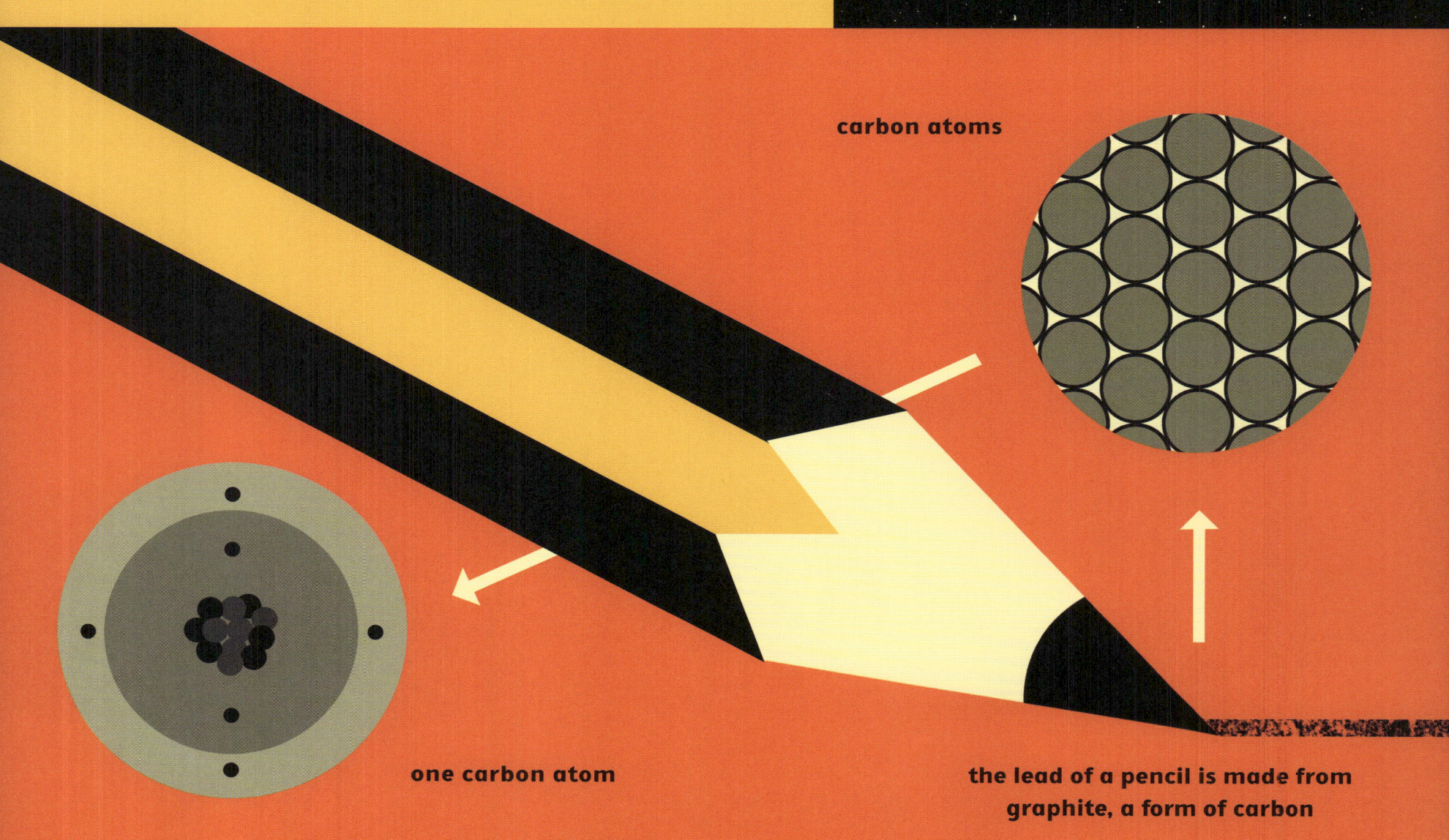

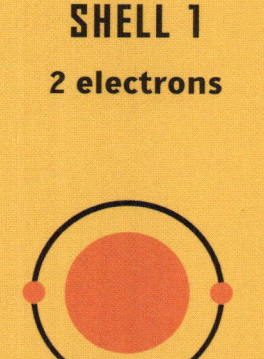

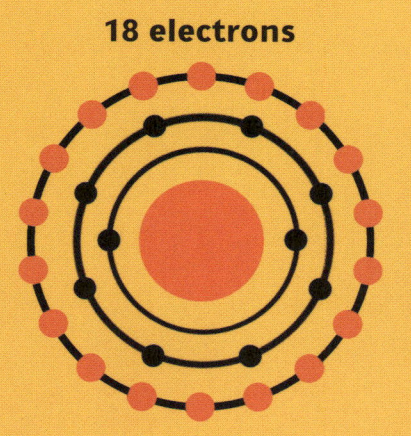

carbon atoms

one carbon atom

the lead of a pencil is made from graphite, a form of carbon

SHELL 1
2 electrons

SHELL 2
8 electrons

SHELL 3
18 electrons

Electrons are huddled together around the nucleus in groups called SHELLS. Each shell can only hold a certain number of electrons. In the first shell it's just 2, the second 8 and the third 18. Can you work out the pattern in this sequence? Do you think you can work out the maximum number of electrons that can fit in the fourth shell?

The answer is 32. There is a **mathematical rule that tells us how many electrons can fit in a particular shell** – it is 2[n x n]. All you have to do is change **n** for the shell number you're looking at, so for the fourth shell it would be 2(4 x 4) = 32. If all four shells of the atom are full it would have **60 electrons in total** (2 + 8 + 18 + 32). However, big atoms don't always fill up their shells. They're more stable (less likely to break apart) if they spread their electrons out. Let's look at **NEODYMIUM** – a soft metal used to make very strong magnets. You'll find its 60 electrons spread out over six shells, arranged 2, 8, 18, 22, 8, 2. The largest atom is **OGANESSON [Og]**, with 118 electrons in seven shells.

Atom Patterns and the Periodic Table

In the heart of an atom is the nucleus, which is made up of particles called **PROTONS** and **NEUTRONS**. Usually an atom has the same number of protons as it does electrons (page 36). The **number of protons** is known as the atom's **ATOMIC NUMBER**.

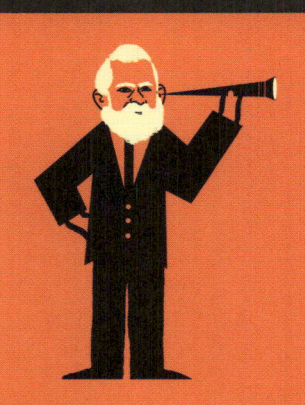

In 1864, English chemist **JOHN NEWLANDS** spotted a pattern hidden within the elements. He noticed that **the properties of a substance are similar in every eighth element**. So **LITHIUM** (3) is similar to **SODIUM** (11) and **POTASSIUM** (19). This pattern is known as the **LAW OF OCTAVES**.

1 H Hydrogen						
3 Li Lithium	4 Be Beryllium					
11 Na Sodium	12 Mg Magnesium					
19 K Potassium	20 Ca Calcium	21 Sc Scandium	22 Ti Titanium	23 V Vanadium	24 Cr Chromium	25 Mn Manganese
37 Rb Rubidium	38 Sr Strontium	39 Y Yttrium	40 Zr Zirconium	41 Nb Niobium	42 Mo Molybdenum	43 Tc Technetium
55 Cs Caesium	56 Ba Barium	57–71 ▼	72 Hf Hafnium	73 Ta Tantalum	74 W Tungsten	75 Re Rhenium
87 Fr Francium	88 Ra Radium	89–103 ▼	104 Rf Rutherfordium	105 Db Dubnium	106 Sg Seaborgium	107 Bh Bohrium

Lanthanides: 57 La Lanthanum | 58 Ce Cerium | 59 Pr Praseodymium | 60 Nd Neodymium | 61 Pm Promethium

Actinides: 89 Ac Actinium | 90 Th Thorium | 91 Pa Protactinium | 92 U Uranium | 93 Np Neptunium

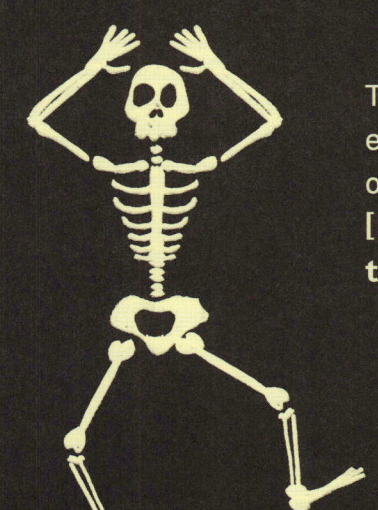

The atomic number is special. It identifies exactly what the atom *is*. For example, gold's atomic number is 79 and silver's is 47. Chemists know of atoms with atomic numbers from 1 [HYDROGEN] all the way up to 118 [OGANESSON]. **If a substance is made up of atoms that all have the same atomic number** it is known as an **ELEMENT**.

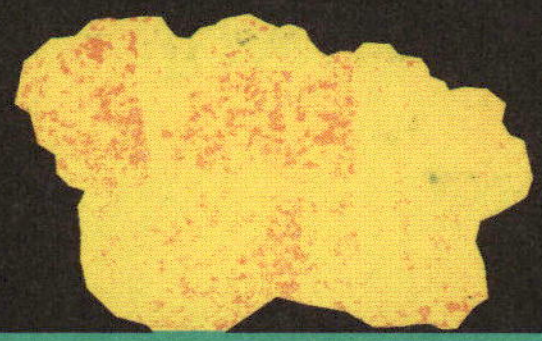

CALCIUM	GOLD	ALUMINIUM	NEON
(20)	(79)	(13)	(10)

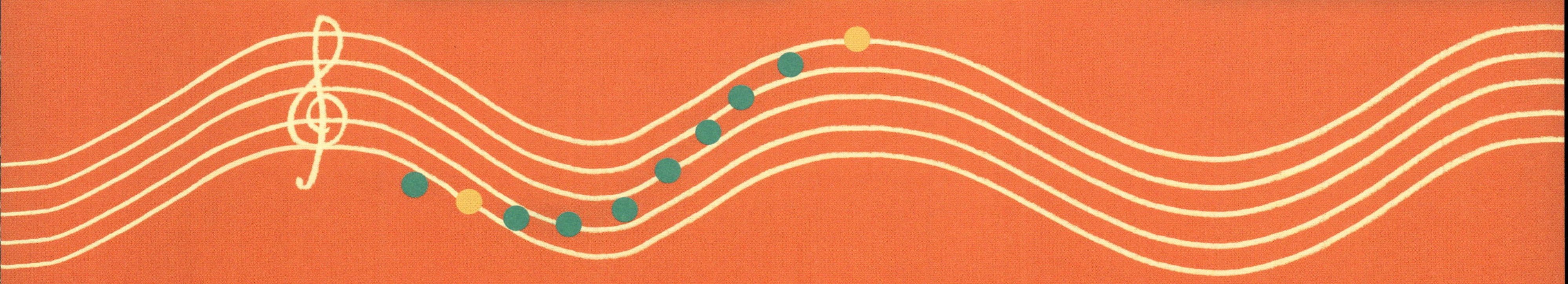

In 1869, Russian scientist **DMITRI MENDELEEV** used this idea to draw up the **PERIODIC TABLE** – a grid organising the elements into groups according to their repeating properties. He cleverly left gaps in order to keep the pattern going and correctly guessed that these were new elements yet to be discovered (such as gallium, germanium and scandium).

So spotting hidden patterns can help you make new discoveries.

39

Getting the Hang of Half-Lifes

Some atoms are like werewolves or vampires – they are able to change into something else. Although, unlike these creatures, it is very hard for them to change back again. They are called **RADIOACTIVE ATOMS**.

ALPHA DECAY

2 protons, 2 neutrons

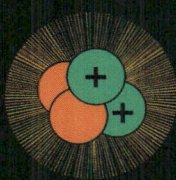

nucleus

Remember, **the number of protons in an atom's nucleus tells you what element it is**. If a nucleus loses or gains protons then it is no longer the same element. Sometimes the nucleus of a radioactive atom becomes unstable and spits out two protons and two neutrons [ALPHA DECAY]. Other times, a neutron suddenly changes into a proton and an electron [BETA DECAY]. This gives the nucleus an extra proton, meaning it shape-shifts into the next element in the periodic table. The atom 'burps out' the spare electron (along with an anti-neutrino).

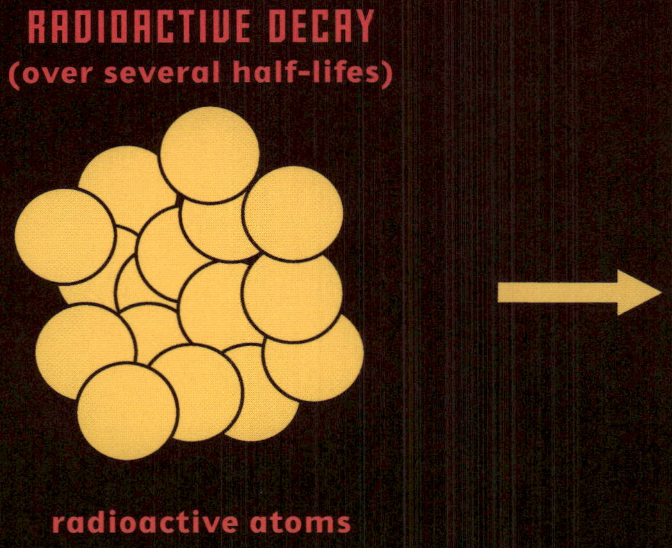

RADIOACTIVE DECAY
(over several half-lifes)

radioactive atoms

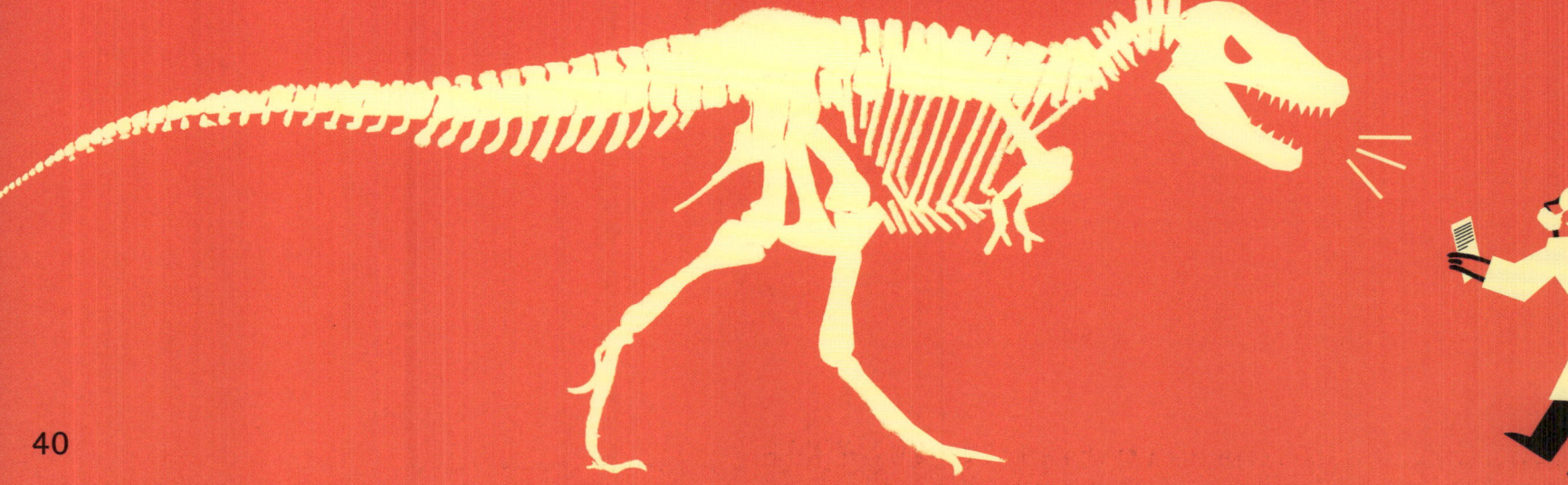

BETA DECAY

electron

anti-neutrino

The strange thing is that it's impossible to predict when a radioactive atom will morph into a different one. However, we do know **how long it takes for half of the atoms in an object to change** – but not which half. This measure of time is called the HALF-LIFE. Sometimes half-lifes are very short – OXYGEN-22 has a half-life of just over two seconds. Yet for URANIUM-238 it's nearly 4.5 billion years! (The numbers after the elements refer to the combined number of protons and neutrons in their atoms).

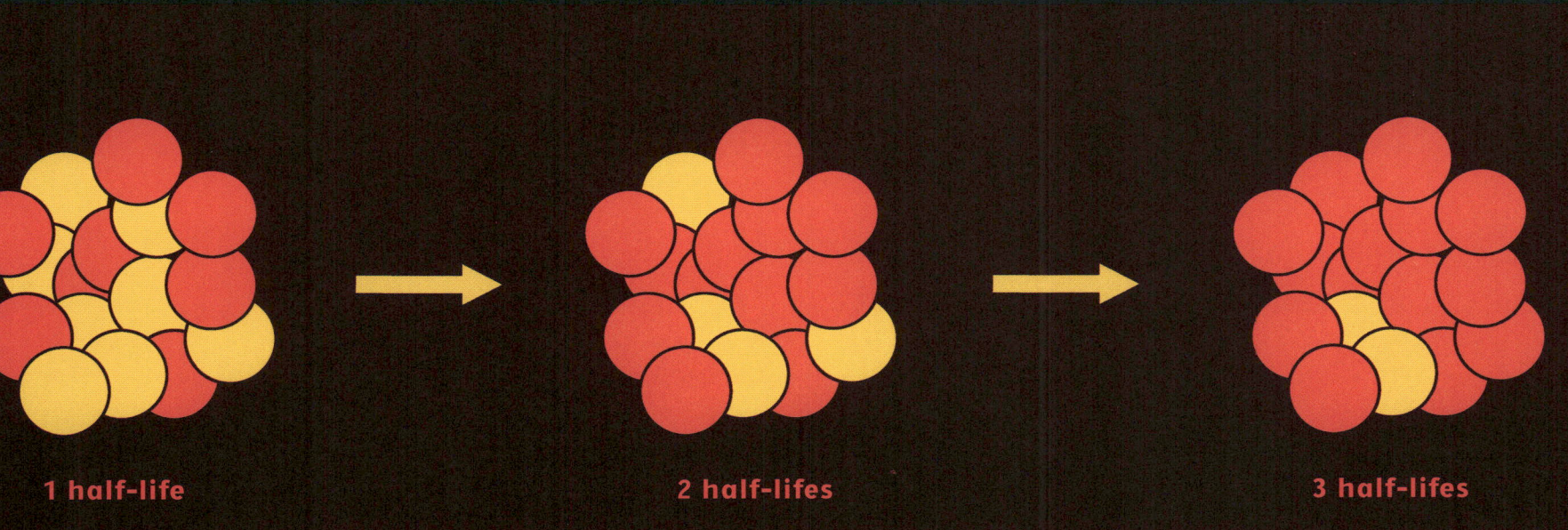

1 half-life → 2 half-lifes → 3 half-lifes

Scientists use half-lifes to work out the age of really old things. Count how many of an object's atoms have 'shape-shifted' and you can work backwards to calculate how long ago the whole decay process started.

Learning the Laws of Gases

Even the air has maths hidden inside it. Every breath involves numbers.

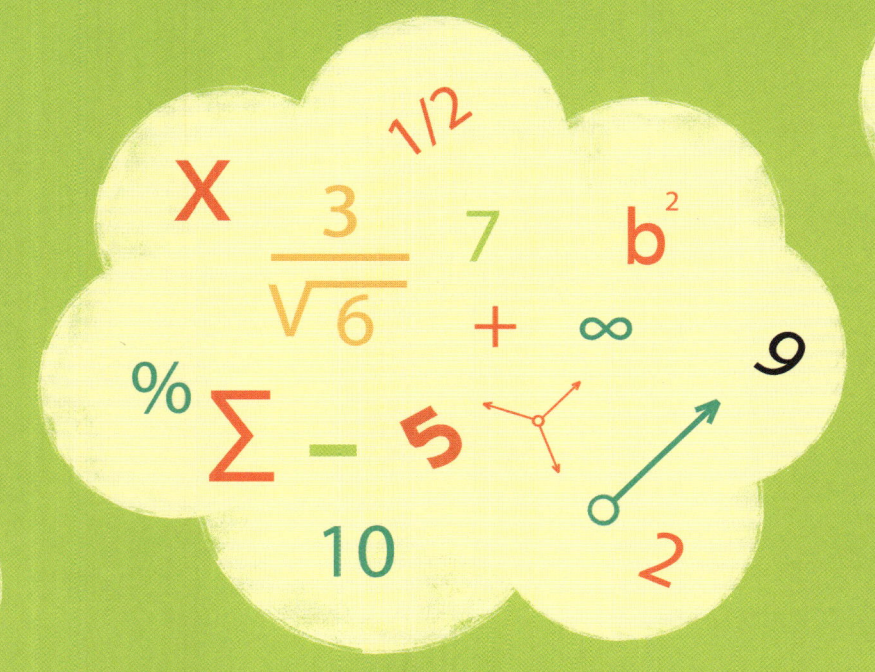

A gas such as air can be described in several ways. You can talk about its **VOLUME – how much space it takes up**, or its **TEMPERATURE – how hot or cold it is**. But a gas also has **PRESSURE – how much force it creates on a particular area**. All these things are related by mathematical laws of nature discovered by different scientists as far back as the 1600s.

air molecules

BOYLE'S LAW
Decrease in volume = increase in pressure

In the 1660s, chemist **ROBERT BOYLE** found that when you **multiply the pressure of a particular gas by its volume you always get the same number** (as long as you keep the temperature the same). This means that if you decrease one, the other increases by exactly the same amount. So if you halve the volume of a gas you double its pressure. This is known as **BOYLE'S LAW**.

CHARLES'S LAW
Increase in temperature = increase in volume

GAY-LUSSAC'S LAW
Increase in temperature = increase in pressure

CHARLES'S LAW, discovered by French scientist **JACQUES CHARLES** in 1787, says that **a gas's volume divided by its temperature will also always give you the same number** (if you don't change its pressure). That means if you double its temperature the volume also doubles.

The same is true of pressure and temperature (without changing the volume) – increase one and the other increases by the same amount. This is known as **GAY-LUSSAC'S LAW** after French chemist **JOSEPH LOUIS GAY-LUSSAC**.

43

Thinking About Time

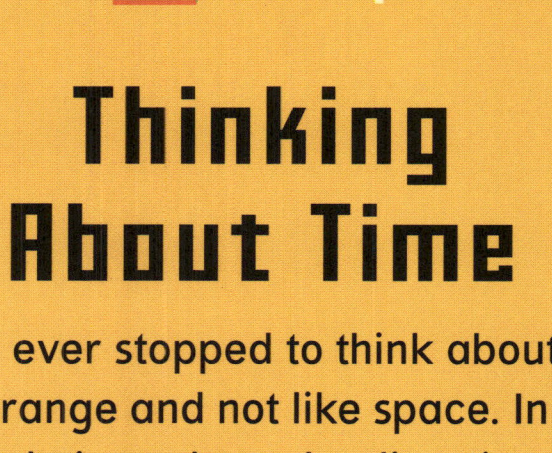

Have you ever stopped to think about **TIME**? Time is strange and not like space. In **SPACE** you have choices about the direction you can travel in. You can walk one way and, if you change your mind, turn around and go back the way you came. Time is very different.

With time you're always racing into the future. You can't travel back to your past again (unless you have a time machine hidden away somewhere!). Scientists say that **time has an arrow – it always points in the same direction, from past to future**.

PAST

That means **things always happen in a certain order**. A hot cup of coffee left alone will always get colder (cold coffee doesn't suddenly get hotter by itself). Bedrooms that aren't tidied will always get messier. Clothes don't suddenly find their way back into the wardrobe. **Over time things get more disordered.**

$$S = k \log W$$

Scientists measure disorder using something called **ENTROPY**. Austrian physicist **LUDWIG BOLTZMANN** famously came up with an equation to calculate entropy **(S)**. It says: $S = k \log W$. **k** is a special number called **Boltzmann's constant**, **log** is short for a mathematical calculation called a **LOGARITHM** and **W** is **the total number of ways you can arrange things**. There are more ways to arrange things in a messy bedroom, so the equation says that a messy bedroom has a higher entropy than a tidy one. This equation is so important that it is even carved on Boltzmann's tombstone.

FUTURE

Einstein's Energetic Equation

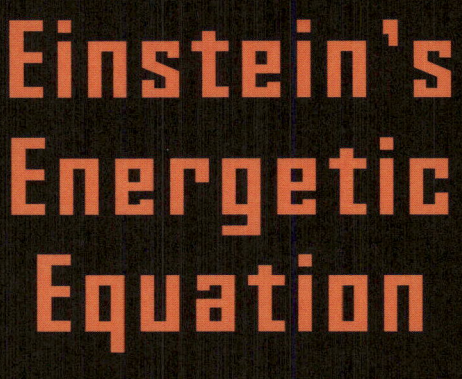

There is no mathematical equation more famous than Einstein's $E=mc^2$. Here, the **E stands for energy**, the **m for mass** and **c^2 for the speed of light multiplied by itself**.

$E=mc^2$

What Einstein is really saying here is that **energy and mass are the same thing** — two sides of a coin. You can turn energy into mass and mass into energy. That's exactly how the **SUN** is powered — deep in its core mass is turned into light energy.

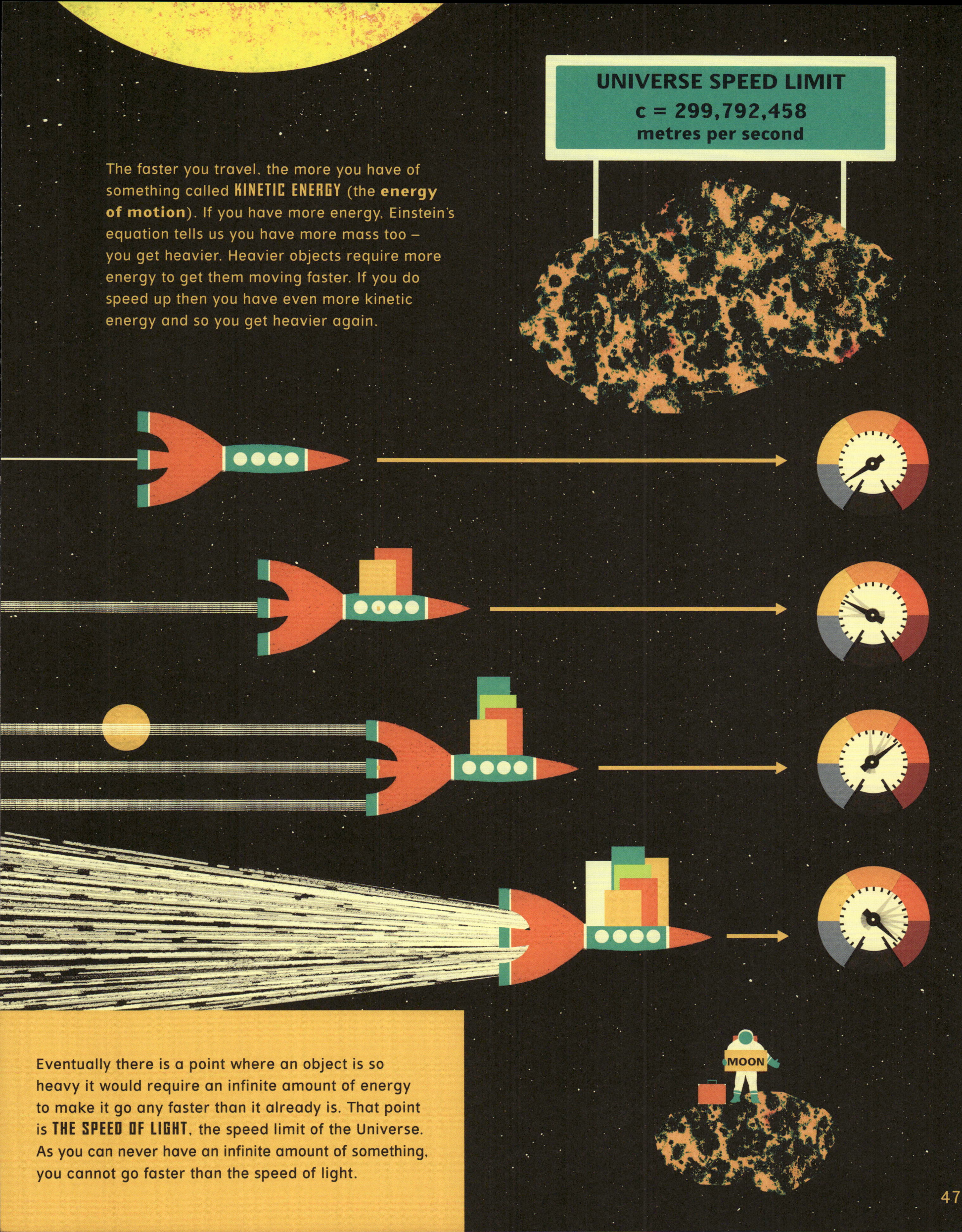

UNIVERSE SPEED LIMIT
c = 299,792,458 metres per second

The faster you travel, the more you have of something called **KINETIC ENERGY** (the **energy of motion**). If you have more energy, Einstein's equation tells us you have more mass too – you get heavier. Heavier objects require more energy to get them moving faster. If you do speed up then you have even more kinetic energy and so you get heavier again.

Eventually there is a point where an object is so heavy it would require an infinite amount of energy to make it go any faster than it already is. That point is **THE SPEED OF LIGHT**, the speed limit of the Universe. As you can never have an infinite amount of something, you cannot go faster than the speed of light.

MOON

The Secrets of Circuits

Picture a world without electricity. No light bulbs to illuminate the darkness, no television to entertain us, no smartphones or cinemas. Every time you flick a switch or plug something in there is maths working hard to keep the power on.

Like cars zooming around a race track, it is **electrons flowing around wires in electric circuits** that provide us with **ELECTRICITY**. Their **speed** is measured by something called the **ELECTRIC CURRENT**. Like a current of water in a river, a stronger electric current means the electricity is flowing faster. Current is measured in **AMPERES**. One ampere of electrical current means **6 million trillion electrons are flowing through the wire every second!**

What material the **wire** is made of affects how the current flows along it. Imagine pouring treacle down on a race track. Suddenly the cars would find it much harder to drive around as fast. Scientists call this RESISTANCE. **The higher the resistance, the harder it is for current to flow**.

In the 1800s, German mathematician GEORG OHM discovered the mathematical relationship between current and resistance. If you multiply them together you get the VOLTAGE (a force that pushes electrons around the circuit). This is called OHM'S LAW. Normally the voltage of a plug socket is fixed, so the lower the resistance in a wire, the higher the electric current.

49

Playing with Pendulums and Springs

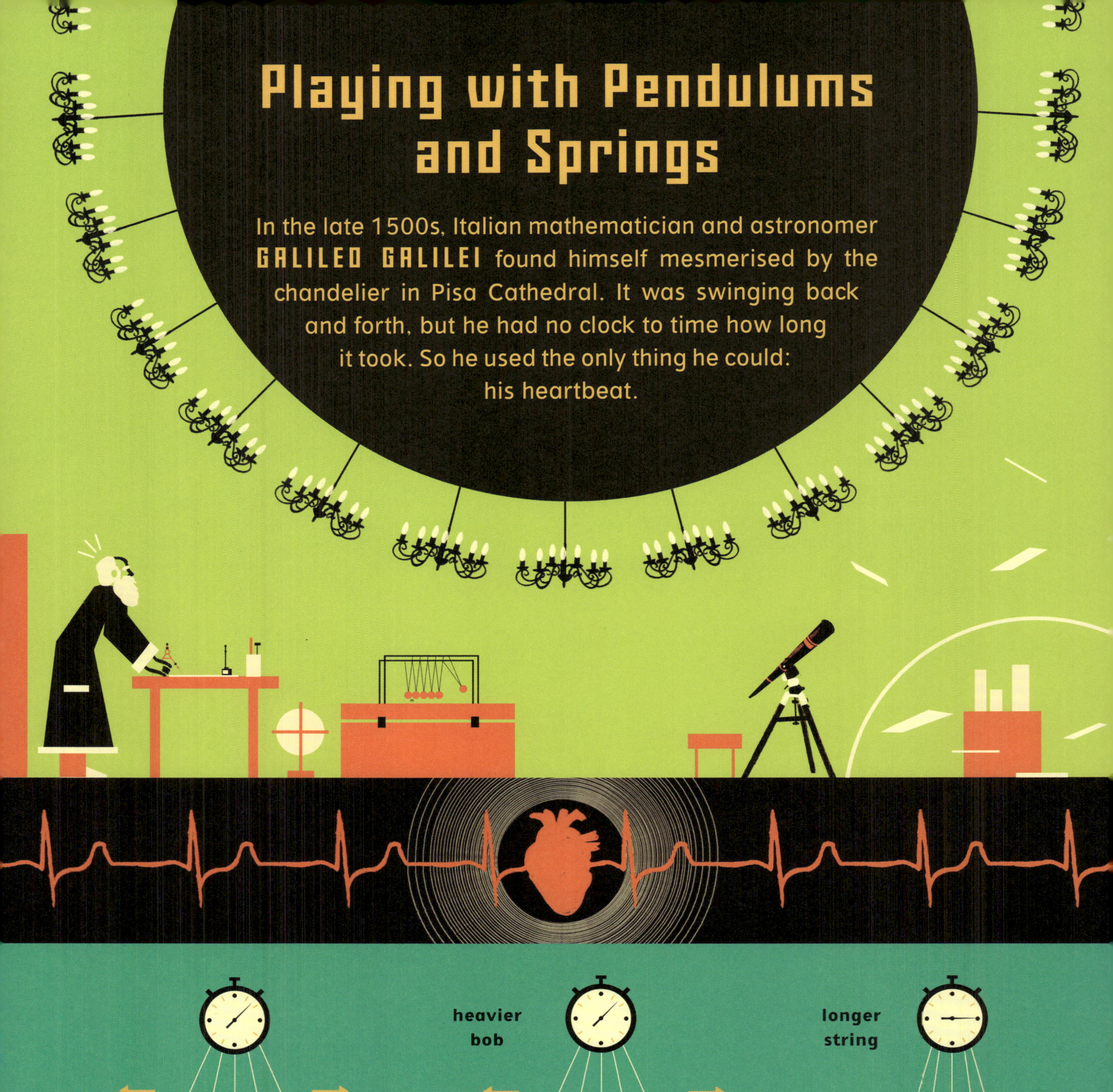

In the late 1500s, Italian mathematician and astronomer **GALILEO GALILEI** found himself mesmerised by the chandelier in Pisa Cathedral. It was swinging back and forth, but he had no clock to time how long it took. So he used the only thing he could: his heartbeat.

heavier bob

longer string

He went on to experiment more with **PENDULUMS – weights (or bobs) swinging on a string**. He was able to show that it isn't the weight of the bob that affects how long it takes a pendulum to swing (the **period**), but the length of the string. Galileo discovered that **the period of a pendulum is linked to the square root of the string length**. The square root of a number is the value that can be multiplied by itself to give the original number. For example, the square root of 4 is 2, because 2 x 2 = 4. So if you make a pendulum four times longer it will take twice as long to swing.

Almost 100 years later, English scientist **ROBERT HOOKE** was investigating what happens if a weight hangs on a spring rather than a rope. He used **a special number to describe the springiness of a spring**, known as k (or the SPRING CONSTANT). Say you want to extend two springs by 5 centimetres. If the second has a spring constant that's double the first, you need to double the force to stretch it by the same amount. This is known as **HOOKE'S LAW**.

The Physics of Floating

Imagine getting so excited by something you discovered in your bathtub that you run out of the house and down the street, shouting at the top of your voice having completely forgotten to put your clothes back on.

. . . Archimedes realised the **water level rises by an amount that's the same as the volume of the object**. If the object is partly submerged then the water only goes up by an amount equal to the volume of the part that's below the waterline.

That's exactly what some people think Greek scientist **ARCHIMEDES** did when he discovered the hidden secrets of how objects displace water. If you **put a heavy object in a bath, it sinks to the bottom and the water level rises** . . .

The weight of that displaced water is important. **ARCHIMEDES'S PRINCIPLE** explains that **an object placed in water – such as a ship – will start to sink until the weight of the water it has displaced is equal to its own weight**. If an object's weight is more than the weight of the water it displaces then it will sink completely. It just goes to show you that discovering something new about the language of the Universe can strike when you least expect it!

EUREKA!

How to Lift with Levers

When was the last time you went to the playground to whizz around on a roundabout, soar on a swing or slip down the slide? If you played on the see-saw you might have noticed something interesting that can be explained by maths.

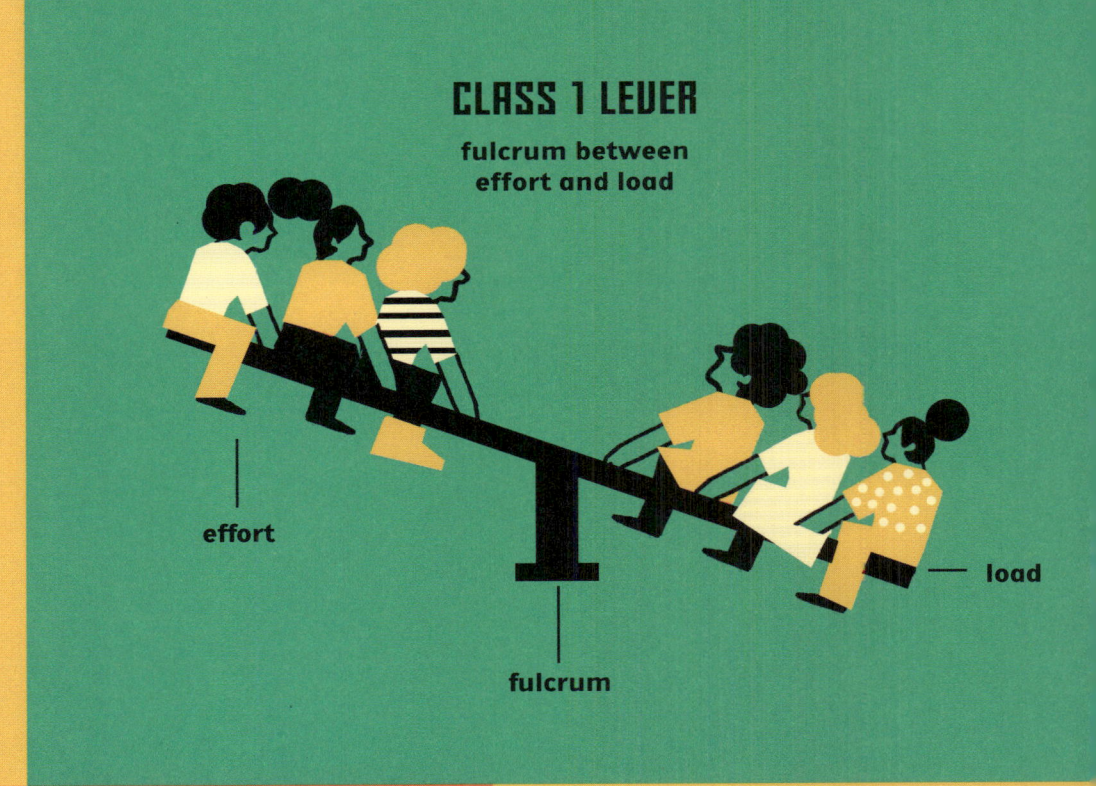

CLASS 1 LEVER
fulcrum between effort and load

effort — fulcrum — load

CLASS 2 LEVER
load between effort and fulcrum

effort — load — fulcrum

If you spotted that someone a different weight to you has to move closer or further away from the middle to keep it balanced, then you already know how levers work without even realising it! Archimedes is not only known for supposedly running down the street naked (page 52), he is also quoted as saying "Give me a lever long enough, and a fulcrum on which to place it, and I shall move the world". A **FULCRUM** is **the point about which a lever turns**, just like the middle of a see-saw (sometimes it's also called the **pivot**). There are three types, or classes, of lever.

CLASS 3 LEVER
effort between load and fulcrum

load — effort — fulcrum

So how can you still lift the other person on the see-saw if they are heavier than you? If you **make the distance between you and the fulcrum longer**, then the **less effort** you have to put in to lift them.

A heavier person can **shorten their distance to the fulcrum** to make them **balance** with a lighter person. If they're twice as heavy they have to halve their distance.

Based on these rules, Archimedes was saying that if he had a lever long enough (and a pivot point) he could even use it to lift up the Earth. Except it wouldn't really work – the Earth is so heavy that his lever would have to be billions of light years long!

Putting Pythagoras into Practice

Sweating under the intense heat of the Sun, huge teams of people worked to build one of the wonders of the ancient world. But have you ever wondered how the Egyptians managed to get the corners of their pyramids so perfectly square?

It's all to do with **PYTHAGORAS'S THEOREM** and **RIGHT-ANGLED TRIANGLES**. Imagine taking some rope and tying knots in it to create 12 equal sections then using the knotted rope to make a triangle with a 90-degree (right) angle and knots at each corner. You'd see that the two straight sides of the triangle have three and four sections along them and the **diagonal side** (called the **HYPOTENUSE**) has five.

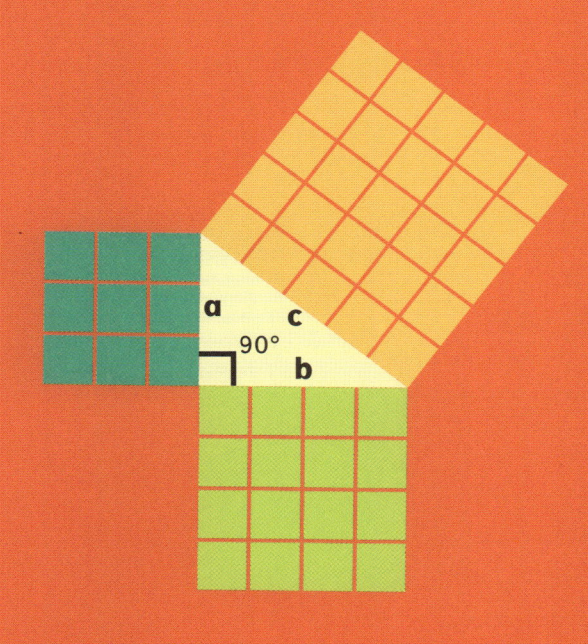

PYTHAGORAS'S THEOREM compares **a, b** and **c – the lengths of the three sides of any triangle with a right-angled corner**. It says that $a^2+b^2=c^2$. Remember that ^{2} means squared, or multiplying a number by itself. This equation is a quicker way of saying (a x a) + (b x b) = (c x c). Try it with 3 as a, 4 as b and 5 as c (c is always the hypotenuse). The ancient Egyptians knew that if they made a triangle with sides obeying this rule then a perfect 90-degree corner was guaranteed.

This theory can also help you get places more quickly. Say you want to get from one corner of a football pitch to the opposite corner. What's quicker? Up one side and along the other or diagonally across? Pythagoras tells us that the diagonal is always shorter than the two sides added together.

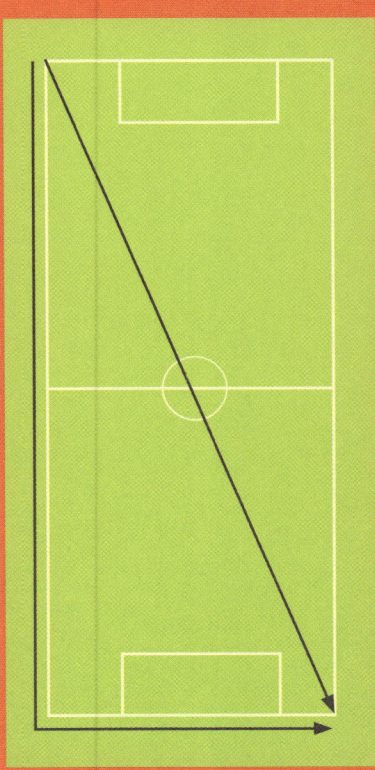

57

Reflecting on Refraction

Have you ever been in the bath with your hands in the water and noticed that your fingers look like they have shrunk? Perhaps you've seen a pencil appearing bent or broken when it's half in and half out of a glass of water? These illusions are light playing a trick on us.

Pull your hand or the pencil out of the water and nothing has really happened to them. The distortion you could see is due to light travelling through two different substances – air and water – at different speeds. The light slows down when it hits the water, causing it to travel at a different angle than before.

When light is bent like this it is called **REFRACTION**. Every substance has a number known as its **REFRACTIVE INDEX** (normally given the letter **n**). The higher a substance's number, the more it bends light. For air, n = 1.0003 and for water, n = 1.33, so you can see why light slows down and bends as it moves from the air to the water.

REFRACTIVE INDEX

VACUUM
n = 1

AIR
n = 1.0003

ICE
n = 1.31

In the 1600s, Dutch astronomer and mathematician **WILLEBRORD SNELLIUS** discovered the link between the angles of bent light as it travels between two substances and the refractive indexes of those materials. **The bigger the difference between the two refractive indexes, the more the light is bent.** This is called **SNELL'S LAW**.

line of sight

angle 1

air
water

illusion fish

angle 2

real fish

WATER	OLIVE OIL	DIAMOND
n = 1.33	n = 1.47	n = 2.42

Kepler's Clockwork Planets

There once was a man who lived in a castle on a tiny island between Sweden and Denmark. His name was **TYCHO BRAHE** and he was so passionate about maths that he lost the tip of his nose in a sword fight with his third cousin over a mathematical formula. For the rest of his life he wore a metal nose!

From his castle, Brahe looked up into the night sky and kept careful records of the positions of the stars and the planets. After his death, his assistant **JOHANNES KEPLER** searched through all the numbers looking for mathematical patterns in the planets. He soon discovered there are **three rules about the way planets orbit the Sun**. They are now known as **KEPLER'S LAWS**.

KEPLER'S FIRST LAW

The shape of a planet's orbit is not a circle. Instead, a planet orbits in an **oval-like shape** called an ELLIPSE.

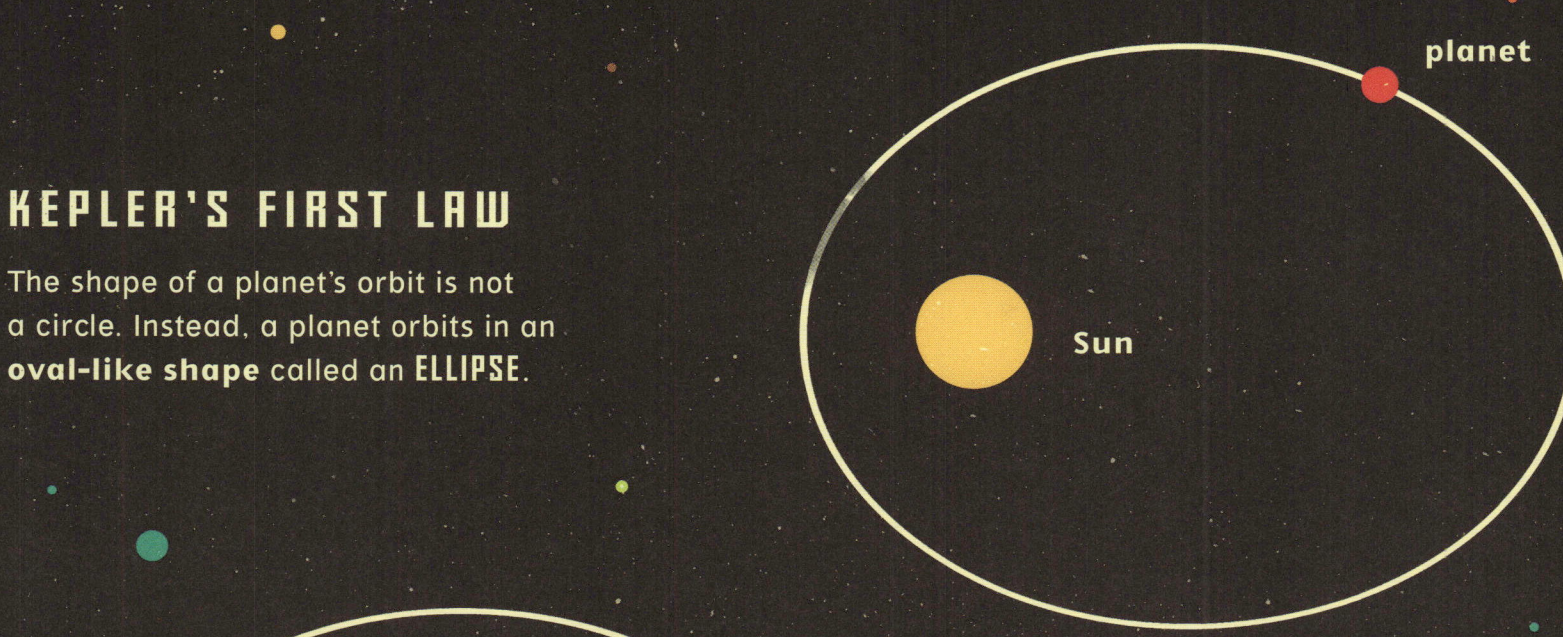

planet

Sun

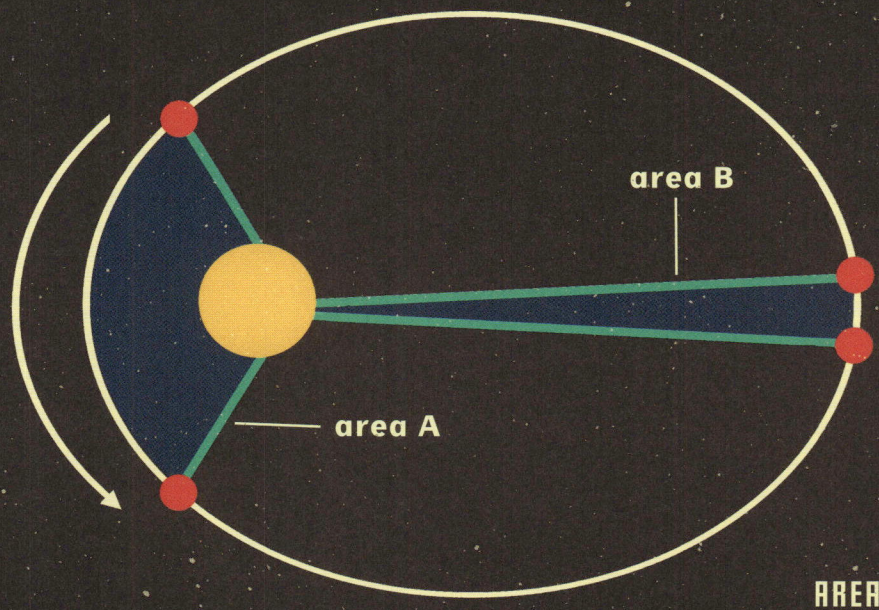

area B

KEPLER'S SECOND LAW

An imaginary line drawn between the Sun and an orbiting planet will always sweep over an equal area in an equal amount of time. This means planets speed up when closer to the Sun and slow down when further away.

area A

AREA A = AREA B

KEPLER'S THIRD LAW

A planet's orbital time squared (multiplied by itself) is closely linked to its distance from the Sun cubed (multiplied by itself twice). So more distant planets take longer to orbit the Sun than closer ones.

Nailing Gravity with Newton

Kepler wasn't able to explain *why* his laws were true, only that they were. It would take mathematician and physicist **ISAAC NEWTON** to explain what was really going on. Newton was in his mother's garden when he saw an apple fall from a tree and hit the ground. In an instant he realised one of the Universe's most important mathematical secrets: **everything is attracted to everything else by a force called GRAVITY**.

The gravity of the Earth pulls apples downwards, but it is also pulling the Moon around us. In turn, the Sun is heaving us and the rest of the planets in the Solar System in orbits around it. After a lot of work Newton came up with a mathematical equation called his **UNIVERSAL LAW OF GRAVITATION**. It says that **the gravitational attraction between two objects is stronger the closer they are**. Newton's equation is known as an **INVERSE SQUARE LAW**. So if you were to double the distance between the Earth and the Moon, for example, their gravitational attraction would drop (because it is inverse) to a quarter (a half squared, or $½^2$).

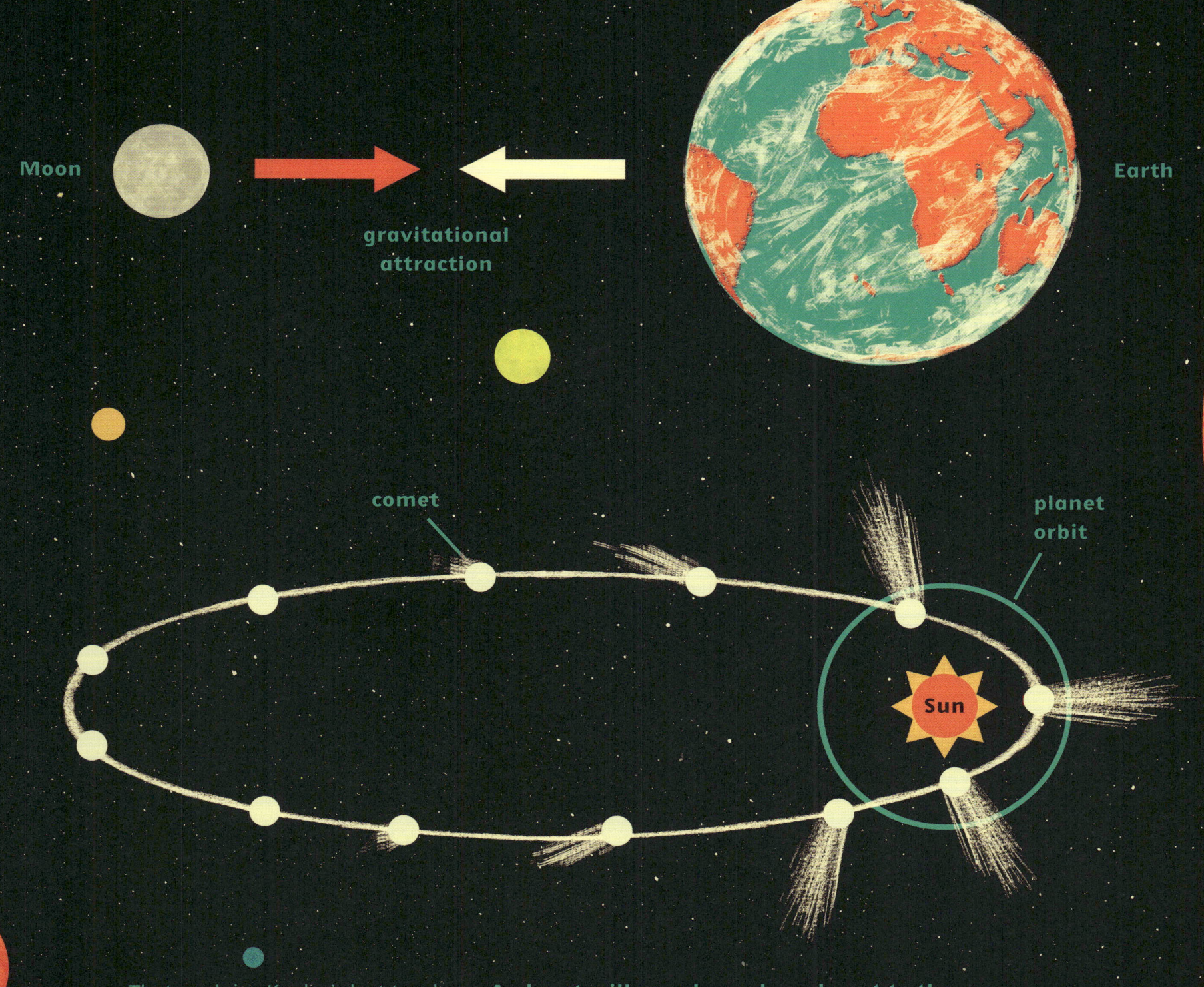

Moon

gravitational attraction

Earth

comet

planet orbit

Sun

That explains Kepler's last two laws. **A planet will speed up when closest to the Sun because it feels more gravitational attraction and it will slow down as it moves away because it feels less** (Second Law). **More distant planets will orbit slower than closer ones because they feel a weaker pull of gravity from the Sun** (Third Law). Observing icy objects called comets as they orbit the Sun was an early way to show Newton's equation was correct. A comet's orbit is much more elliptical that a planet's, plunging it from the furthest reaches of the Solar System to close to the Sun.

Hurtling Through Space with Hubble

Where did the Universe come from? It is one of the biggest questions you can ask about the world around you. The man who gave us part of the answer to this was American astronomer EDWIN HUBBLE.

In the 1920s, Hubble was studying **big groups of stars in space** called GALAXIES. He wanted to know two things about each galaxy: how far away it is and how fast it is moving. After carefully making those measurements he found something extraordinary. **Almost every galaxy in the Universe is moving away from us**. What's more, the furthest galaxies appear to be flying away the fastest.

Hubble summed this up in an equation known as **HUBBLE'S LAW**:

$$V = H_0 \times d$$

V is a galaxy's speed and **d is its distance from us**. H_0 **is a number called Hubble's constant**, which is always the same. So Hubble's Law tells us that the larger a galaxy's distance is (d), the higher the speed it's travelling at (V).

HAPPY 14,000,000,000TH BIRTHDAY!

If everything is moving away from us now, it must have been closer together in the past. Keep working backwards and you'll find **the point when the expansion started**. Astronomers call this the **BIG BANG** and it happened nearly 14 billion years ago. You can get this number by dividing 1 by Hubble's constant.

Dealing with Distances in Space

How exactly do you measure distances in space? It's not like you can reach out into the Solar System and beyond with a big ruler. The answer – of course – is maths.

Earth's position in June

Earth's position in December

One way of measuring cosmic distances is called **PARALLAX** and it works like this. Close one eye and hold up your finger at arm's length. Line you finger up with the line that separates these two pages. Then change the eye that's open. What happened? You should see your finger jump across on to one of the pages. Remember where your finger landed.

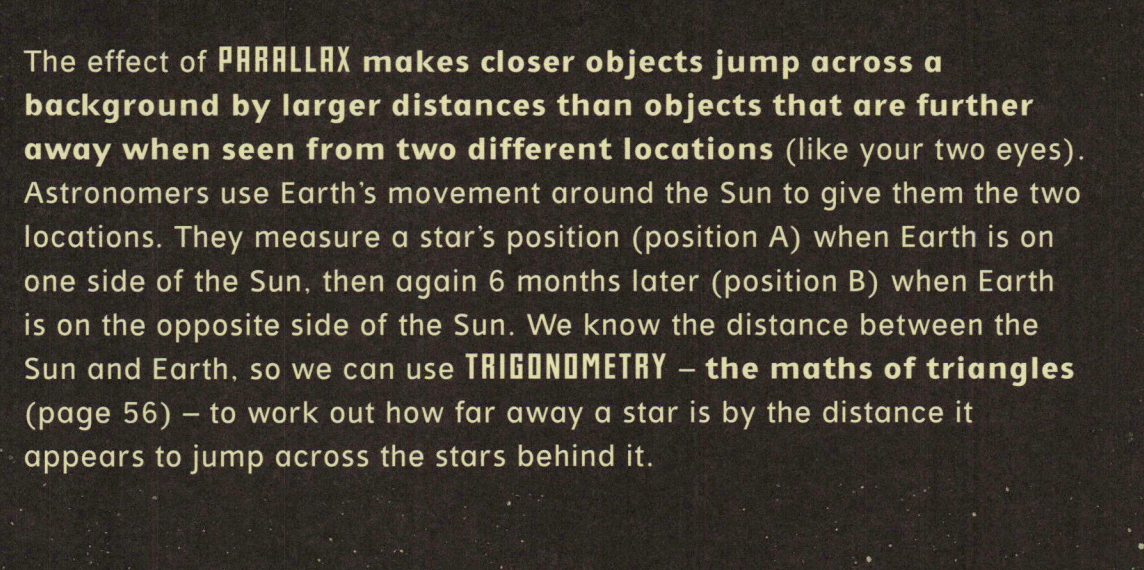

The effect of **PARALLAX** makes closer objects jump across a background by larger distances than objects that are further away when seen from two different locations (like your two eyes). Astronomers use Earth's movement around the Sun to give them the two locations. They measure a star's position (position A) when Earth is on one side of the Sun, then again 6 months later (position B) when Earth is on the opposite side of the Sun. We know the distance between the Sun and Earth, so we can use **TRIGONOMETRY** – **the maths of triangles** (page 56) – to work out how far away a star is by the distance it appears to jump across the stars behind it.

position A

star

position B

The European Space Agency's *Gaia* telescope is using this technique to measure the distances to a billion stars.

Now do the same thing again, but start with your finger much closer to your face. When you change the eye that's open does your finger jump more or less than before? It should be more.

67

Let's Talk Technological Change

The world has undergone huge change thanks to the explosion of computer technology. Computers work by doing calculations on small computer chips packed full of devices called transistors. In the 1960s engineer GORDON MOORE predicted that the number of transistors we could cram on to a computer chip would double every two years. Mathematicians call this EXPONENTIAL GROWTH. In 1985, two Nintendo games consoles were as powerful as the computer that guided the Apollo 11 astronauts all the way to the Moon just 16 years earlier in 1969.

1950
1 transistor

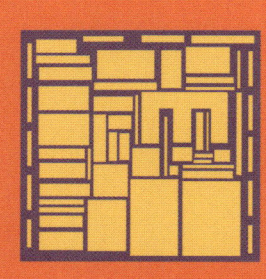

1980s
275,000 transistors

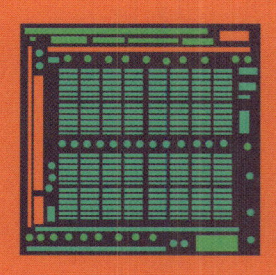

2010s
8 billion transistors

printing press
1440s

telescope
1608

light bulb
1800s

To understand the power of exponential growth, imagine that for every lie Pinocchio tells, his nose grows by an amount that's double the amount before. The first time he fibs it grows 5 centimetres, but the second lie sees it grow by another 10 centimetres. He'd only have to tell a total of 33 lies for his nose to stretch all the way to the Moon!

iPad
2000s

mobile phones
1970s

people on
the Moon
1969

Humans have been thinking about the maths of exponential growth for a long time. Around the year 1000, the Persian poet **FIRDAWSI** wrote about placing grains of rice on a chessboard: one grain on the first square, two on the second and four on the third, so that each new square doubles the number of grains of the one before. How many grains would you need to fill up all 64 squares? The answer is:

18,446,744,073,709,551,615

That's nearly 18.5 quintillion – or enough to form a pile larger than Mount Everest!

Calculating with Computers

What if you could only speak two words? You might think your language would be extremely limited, yet computers get by using only two numbers: **0 and 1**. They are known as **b**inary dig**its** or **BITS**.

0100001111111010011100
0000000110100011111000101001111
10101010000110001010100011110001
0001110010101001111000010101
11000101010001111000

You have more in common with a bit than you might think. Throughout your life you are either asleep or awake. Similarly, **a bit can be thought of as either off (0) or on (1)**. The more bits you put together, the more information you can store.

Picture two people called Bowie and Isobel. Between them there are four different possibilities of being awake or asleep: they are both asleep (00), they are both awake (11), Bowie sleeps while Isobel is awake (01), and Bowie is awake while Isobel sleeps (10). Each one is a unique combination of information. The more people you introduce, the higher the number of possible combinations you can describe.

0   0
1   1
0   1
1   0

UNITS OF STORAGE

BIT
single binary digit (1 or 0)

BYTE [B]
8 bits = one character

KILOBYTE [KB]
1,000 bytes = short paragraph

MEGABYTE [MB]
1,000 kilobytes = short novel

GIGABYTE [GB]
1,000 megabytes = 7 minutes of HD video

TERABYTE [TB]
1,000 gigabytes = 50,000 trees' worth of printed paper

PETABYTE [PB]
1,000 terabytes = 20 million 4-drawer filing cabinets filled with printed pages

EXABYTE [EB]
1,000 petabytes = one-fifth of all the words ever spoken by humans

Computers work in a similar way by collecting **eight bits together** to form a **BYTE**. Each bit can be a 0 or a 1, leading to 256 (2^8, or 2 x 2 x 2 x 2 x 2 x 2 x 2 x 2) different ways of storing information in one byte.

You might have heard of **MEGABYTES (a million bytes)** or **GIGABYTES (a billion bytes)**. Modern smartphones can easily hold tens of gigabytes of information, all made up of lots of bits that are either asleep or awake.

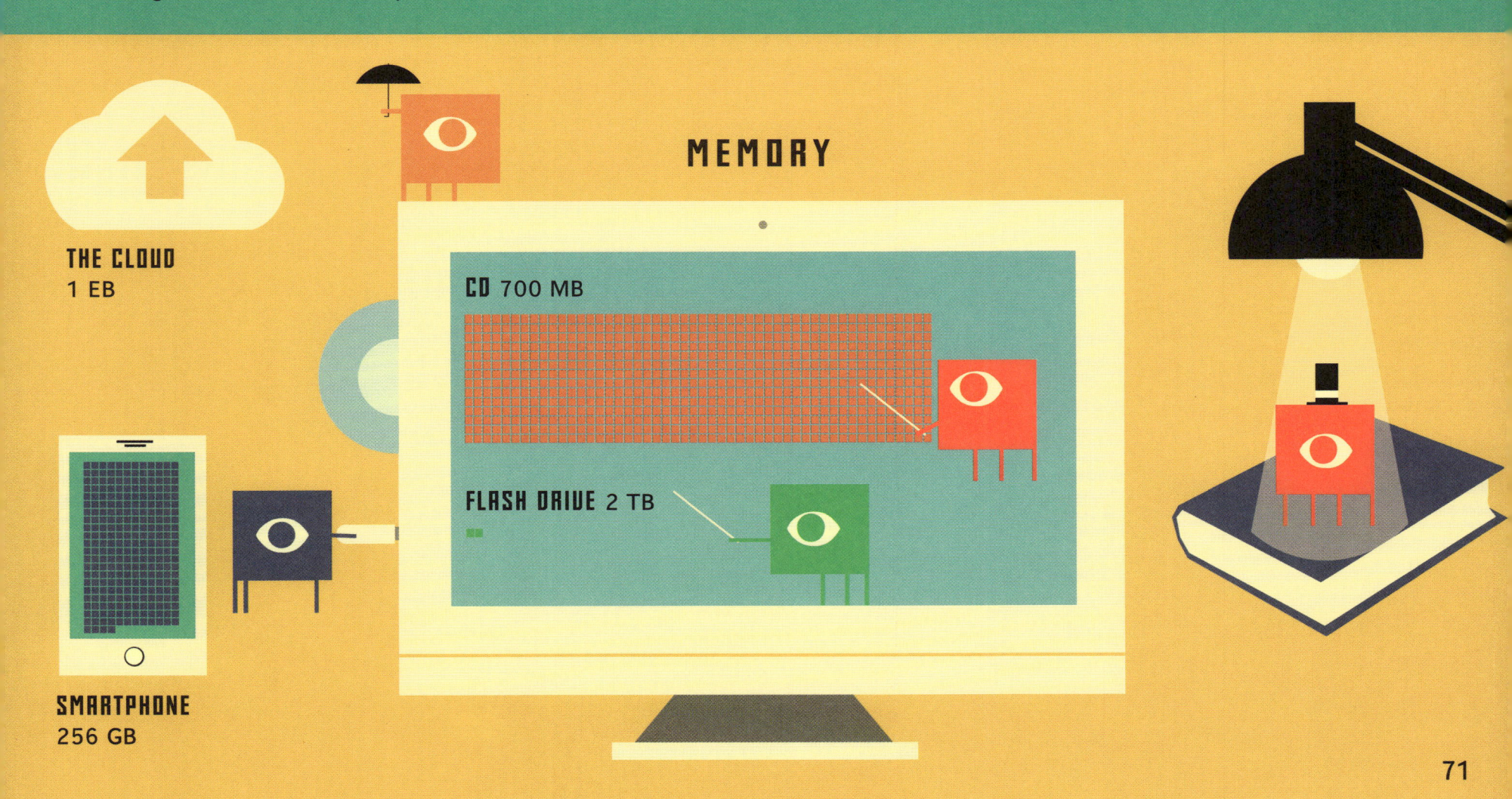

MEMORY

THE CLOUD 1 EB

SMARTPHONE 256 GB

CD 700 MB

FLASH DRIVE 2 TB

Getting Crafty with Cryptography

Imagine if you could see the information flying all around you right now. Every room is flooded with **DATA** – **strings of zeroes and ones** – pinging between connected devices such as computers, smartphones and tablets. But with all this data everywhere, how do you keep your information safe from people who might want to steal it?

Ibjm Dbftbs!

The answer is **ENCRYPTION** – **turning important information into a code that only certain people can crack**. The science of codes is called **CRYPTOGRAPHY** and people have been writing in code for thousands of years. Roman emperor **JULIUS CAESAR** invented a cipher, or code, to keep his messages hidden. He would substitute every letter for the next one along in the alphabet.

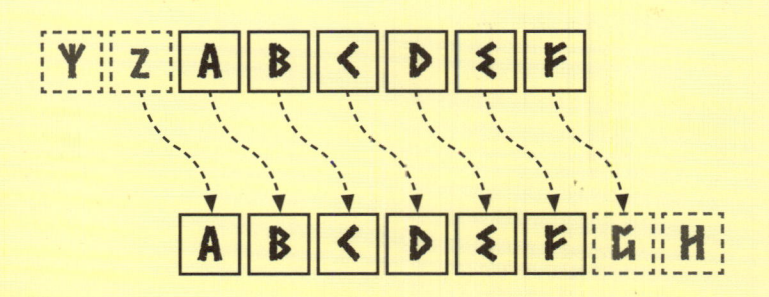

Y Z A B C D E F
↓ ↓ ↓ ↓ ↓ ↓ ↓ ↓
A B C D E F G H

'Hail Caesar!' would become 'Ibjm Dbftbs!'. Only someone who knew the code could easily read his messages.

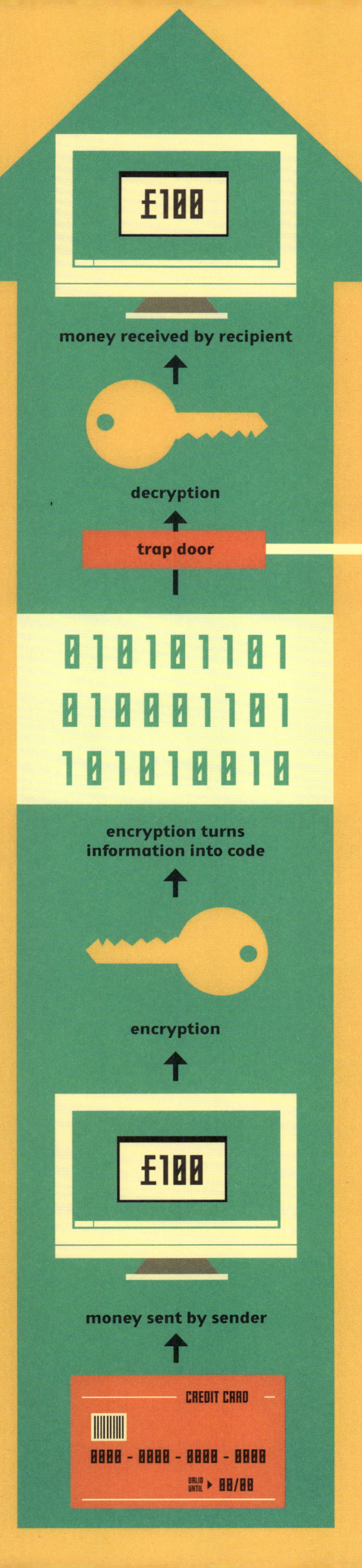

Modern computers can crack the **CAESAR CIPHER** quickly, so encryption on the Internet needs to be a lot more sophisticated. Every time someone buys something online their payment details are turned into a code by multiplying two very big prime numbers together – numbers that can only be divided by themselves and one (page 14). This process is sometimes called a **TRAP DOOR FUNCTION** – it's very easy to go one way (multiplying the primes together) but very hard to go the other (working out which primes have been multiplied). It would take longer than the age of the Universe to crack the code!

£100

money received by recipient

decryption

trap door

01010110 1
01000110 1
10101001 0

encryption turns information into code

encryption

£100

money sent by sender

CREDIT CARD
0000 - 0000 - 0000 - 0000
VALID UNTIL ▶ 00/00

Building the Future with Big Data

In 2017, we created 2.5 quintillion bytes of data every single day. That's more in one year than in the last 5,000 years of human history combined! How long does it take for us to create the same amount of data as every book ever written? Less than a second.

We've never had as much information about the way we live our lives and the world around us as we do now. We are living in the age of **'big data'** and mathematicians are inventing new ways to look through all of it to spot patterns and trends. Scientists create **computer programs** called ALGORITHMS to 'mine' the data for important information.

This is revolutionising the way we treat people for different diseases. If anonymous data about everyone's medical treatments were available all at once, it would be easier to see what works and what doesn't. Analysing big data could save lives by drastically reducing the occurrence of conditions like cancer – or even eliminating them altogether.

In one famous example in 2017, scientists used data generated by social media website Twitter to predict an outbreak of flu six weeks earlier than other methods. They did it by analysing 50 million tweets looking for words like 'coughing' or 'vomiting'.

The World Needs You

We have come a long way since our ancestors ventured down from the trees and started walking on two legs. The marvels of the modern technological world would look like magic to people who lived just a few centuries ago. But it's not magic – it's maths. Our success is built on the realisation that we live in a universe of numbers. **Mathematics is at the heart of everything we do**.

Our past may be impressive, but our future is uncertain. The damage we are doing to the environment means that Earth's climate is changing at an alarming pace. There are more people on the planet than ever before and that only seems set to continue. Working out how to keep everyone alive while still protecting our planet is going to take some incredibly clever thinking. Humans have shown time and again that we are capable of amazing feats of imagination and we're going to need all of it to keep our journey going.

You can be sure that maths will be there to help us. From curing diseases, sending the first people to Mars and inventing artificial intelligence, by learning more about numbers we can improve our outlook. Could you be part of our mathematical quest to build a better future?